Y
940.27
BAL
I

**Balkwill, Richard**
Trafalgar.

# GREAT BATTLES AND SIEGES

# TRAFALGAR
## RICHARD BALKWILL

ILLUSTRATIONS BY
**FRED ANDERSON**

**New York**

Maxwell Macmillan Canada
Toronto

Maxwell Macmillan International
New York • Oxford • Singapore • Sydney

# GREAT BATTLES

First American publication 1993 by New Discovery Books, Macmillan Publishing Company, 866 Third Avenue, New York, NY 10022
Maxwell Macmillan Canada Inc., 1200 Eglinton Avenue East, Suite 200, Don Mills, Ontario M3C 3N1

Macmillan Publishing Company is part of the Maxwell Communication Group of Companies.

First published in 1993 in Great Britain by
Zoë Books Limited
15 Worthy Lane
Winchester
Hampshire SO23 7AB
England

## A ZOË BOOK

Devised and produced by
Zoë Books Limited
15 Worthy Lane
Winchester
Hampshire SO23 7AB
England

Printed in Italy by Grafedit SpA
Design: Julian Holland Publishing, Ltd.
Picture research: Victoria Sturgess
Illustrations: Fred Anderson
Cartography: Gecko Ltd.
Production: Grahame Griffiths

10 9 8 7 6 5 4 3 2 1

Library of Congress Cataloging-in-Publication Data
Balkwill, Richard.
    Trafalgar/Richard Balkwill.
      p. cm.—(Great battles and sieges)
    Includes bibliographical references and index.
    Summary: Describes the noted sea battle in which the English defeated Spanish and French forces and Admiral Horatio Nelson lost his life.
    ISBN 0-02-726326-6
    1. Trafalgar, Battle of, 1805—Juvenile literature. 2. Napoleonic Wars, 1800-1815—Juvenile literature. [1. Trafalgar, Battle of, 1805. 2. Napoleonic Wars, 1800-1815—Campaigns.] I. Title. II. Series.
DA88.5 1805.B35   1993
940.2'745—dc20                                            93.2650

The author and publishers wish to thank the following who have kindly given permission for the use of copyright material:

Alan Schom and Michael Joseph Ltd. for an extract from
*Trafalgar: Countdown to Battle, 1803–1805* by Alan Schom
(New York: Atheneum, 1990; Michael Joseph, 1990)

**Photographic acknowledgments**

The publishers wish to acknowledge, with thanks, the following photographic sources:
Hulton-Deutsch Collection 11; The Mansell Collection 28t; Musée de la Marine, Paris 5; National Maritime Museum, London 8t, 9, 14, 17, 18, 19, 28b; Nelson Museum, Monmouth 8b, 26; Peter Newark's Historical Pictures Cover, 3, 6, 7, 10, 15, 20, 22, 23, 25, 27, 29; courtesy of the Commanding Officer, HMS Victory 13

# TRAFALGAR

# Contents

# The lonely sea

About 16 miles (25 kilometers) to the west of Cape Trafalgar, near the port of Cadiz in southwest Spain, lies the site of one of the most important battles ever fought at sea. Land battles are marked by monuments and memorials, but here there is nothing to mark the spot. Indeed, if you came here by boat today, the surroundings would look just as they did nearly 200 years ago. This is a wild, lonely stretch of ocean. The massive cliffs of Cape Trafalgar, to the east, are just out of sight. Wheeling seabirds fly above the restless swell. The waves of the Atlantic Ocean, sometimes rising to over 30 feet (10 meters), make all but the biggest ships rise and fall uncomfortably.

## A battle lost and won

It was here, on Monday, October 21, 1805, that 27 ships of the British Royal Navy met in battle with a combined French and Spanish **fleet** of 33 ships. The British ships carried about 17,000 men and 2,148 guns. They were commanded by Admiral Lord Nelson from his **flagship**, HMS *Victory*.

The combined fleet of the French and Spanish had many more men— nearly 30,000—and 2,568 guns. It was commanded by the French vice admiral, Pierre Villeneuve, on the *Bucentaure*.

After a five-hour battle, in which 5,000 men died and thousands more were wounded, it was the larger fleet that was forced to surrender. Nineteen ships of the combined fleet were captured or sunk, but the British fleet, although badly damaged, lost no ships.

▶ *This map shows western Europe at the time of the Battle of Trafalgar. The most powerful countries were Britain and France.*

# TRAFALGAR

## Death and destruction at sea

The battle was described as a "glorious victory" for Britain, and it certainly helped to change the course of history. However, there was very little that was glorious about the battle itself. The continuous roar of the cannon, the smoke and flames, and the crashing of sails and masts onto the decks led to the death and **mutilation** of thousands of men. That was the reality of battle.

The small ships of those days, powered only by sails, were at the mercy of the open sea. One day the wind might be too light or blowing from the wrong direction. The next day it might suddenly turn into a destructive gale. Ships were guided only by **compasses** and by **sextants**, instruments that measured the exact position of the ship in relation to the sun and stars.

What was it that caused so many men to risk their lives in such dangerous conditions? Why was the terrible sea battle fought off Cape Trafalgar? The history of the conflict went back many years and involved two remarkable men—the French emperor, Napoleon Bonaparte, and a British admiral named Horatio Nelson.

▼ *Villeneuve's flagship was the* Bucentaure. *Here the ship is shown under full sail, flying the French flag.*

# Europe at war

Great Britain had been fighting wars for much of the eighteenth century and so had its chief rival, France. These two European nations had built up **empires** around the world. They had both seized land in India, the West Indies, and North America. Between 1775 and 1783 Britain lost much of its American territory when local **colonists** arose against British rule. In 1778 the French supported the Americans in their revolution.

## The rise of Napoleon

In 1789 there was also a revolution in France. The French king was overthrown and later executed. The new French **republic** declared war on Britain and in 1794 invaded the Netherlands. In 1795 France made peace with the German state of Prussia and with Spain. In 1796 the French crushed Austria and marched south to invade most of Italy.

The French army was led by a brilliant young soldier named Napoleon Bonaparte. Three years later Napoleon seized control of the French government, and by 1804 he was powerful enough to proclaim himself Emperor of France.

▶ *Napoleon Bonaparte inspects the French fleet at Boulogne. This Channel port was at the center of French plans for an invasion of Britain. The port would not have been an easy place for the French to defend if it had been attacked by Nelson.*

# Trafalgar

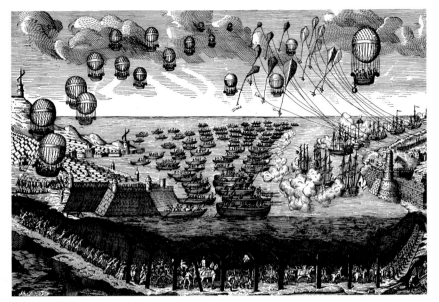

◀ *Napoleon received many wild, fanciful suggestions for invading Britain. In this scene there are balloons and kites and an early form of the Channel Tunnel.*

In the meantime the war had spread like wildfire. Napoleon was prevented from gaining control of Egypt, but he forced Russia, Denmark, and Sweden to join his fight against Britain. When the Danish fleet **blockaded** the Baltic Sea in 1801, it was overpowered by the British vice admiral Horatio Nelson at the Battle of Copenhagen. Europe was weary of war, and a peace agreement was signed at Amiens, France, in 1802. It did not last long.

By 1803 Britain was terrified of Napoleon. Surely he now aimed to control all Europe? Would he soon invade the British Isles from northern France? Large French armies had already been moved to ports such as Boulogne, and all kinds of plans were being made to carry them across the English Channel. In the face of public panic, Britain declared war on France. France demanded support from Spain, in the form of men and money, and in 1804 Spain, too, joined the war.

## Atlantic chase

One of Napoleon's many plans was to send a French navy to the West Indies. There it could attack British-ruled islands. The British fleet would then be forced to sail to defend the West Indies. The French could hurry back across the Atlantic Ocean, join with the Spanish fleet, and attack the English coast.

The plan did not work out. The British, under Admiral William Cornwallis, blockaded a large part of the French fleet in the port of Brest. Another part of the French fleet was forced to stay in Toulon, in southern France. There they stayed for months on end, underfed and poorly supplied. The crews' spirits sank very low.

In the end the French did sail for the West Indies, and Nelson followed them. However, on their return they were met by the English vice admiral Sir Robert Calder. The French turned south to join the Spanish forces in Cadiz.

# Horatio Nelson

The Battle of Trafalgar made Horatio Nelson one of the most famous men in British history. He was born on September 29, 1758, at Burnham Thorpe in Norfolk, England. His father, Edmund, was the village **rector**. The young Horace, as he was then known, was small and weak. Even as an adult he was only 5 ft 6 in (1.7 meters) tall. As a child, Horace doted on his mother, but she died when he was nine. The grief he felt stayed with him strongly all his life.

## The young volunteer

Edmund Nelson had eight children. He now struggled to raise them single-handedly. At Christmas 1770 young Horace and his brother William read some exciting news in the local newspaper. Their uncle, Captain Maurice Suckling, was taking command of a 64-gun ship, the *Raisonnable*, which had been captured from the French.

Horace persuaded his brother to write to their father, who was in Bath, "and tell him I should like to go with my uncle Maurice to sea." He eventually joined his uncle's ship at Chatham in March 1771.

Captain Suckling's reaction was interesting, if not prophetic. "What has poor Horatio done who is so weak that he, above all the rest, should be sent to rough it out at sea? But let him come and the first time we go into action a cannon ball may knock off his head and provide for him at once."

Not yet 13 years old, Horatio Nelson began the hard life of a **midshipman**.

▲ *The young Lieutenant Horatio Nelson boards and captures an enemy ship. His abilities were soon noticed by senior officers.*

▶ *Burnham Thorpe, in Norfolk, was the birthplace of Horace (Horatio) Nelson in 1758. His father, Edmund, was the local rector.*

# TRAFALGAR

## Learning the ropes

On his uncle's ship, Nelson learned all the basic facts about ships and the sea. Very early in his naval career, he sailed on a **merchantman** to the West Indies. He learned how to **navigate** and how to handle the **rigging** and the ship's boats. Above all, he learned what it was like to live the life of an ordinary seaman. This helped him later in life to earn the respect of his crews.

Nelson's first naval command was of the **tender** to HMS *Triumph*. Based in the **estuary** of the Thames River, he learned the difficult skills of handling a boat in changing winds and tides and of **maneuvering** in a restricted space.

## To the West Indies

After a visit to the Arctic and a spell of service in the West Indies, Horatio Nelson was appointed **post-captain**. It was 1779 and he was only 21. While in the West Indies, he met a young widow named Frances Nesbit. She lived on the island of Nevis with her young son. She and Nelson were married in 1787, and they returned to live in the rectory at Burnham Thorpe.

Five years of peace followed. Nelson did not enjoy having nothing to do, and it seems that his wife did not enjoy the quiet life and cold climate of the East Anglian countryside. They later separated.

## Bravery and honor

When war with France broke out in 1793, Nelson took part in many actions. At the siege of Calvi, in Corsica in 1794, he lost sight in one eye after a shell exploded near his face and showered him with splinters. In 1797 near Santa Cruz de Tenerife, he tried to capture a Spanish treasure ship. A **musket** ball smashed his right arm, which had to be **amputated** below the shoulder.

Nelson always took risks and showed great daring. He sometimes ignored orders and was criticized for disobedience. However, this did lead to brilliant successes on many occasions. At the Battle of Copenhagen in 1801 his commander signaled for the battle to stop. Nelson, raising his telescope to his blind eye, said "I really do not see the signal." He went on fighting and within an hour had won a victory for Britain.

Nelson was promoted to commodore, rear admiral, and then commander in chief. He was honored by the nation, becoming Sir Horatio Nelson in 1797 and Lord Nelson in 1798.

## Love in Naples

In 1799 Nelson met Emma, Lady Hamilton. She was the wife of Sir William Hamilton, who was the British ambassador in Naples, Italy. All three liked one another, but soon Emma and Nelson were having a passionate and reckless love affair.

The world knew of the affair, but its details were kept secret. The couple had a daughter, Horatia, who was born in 1801. Horatia lived to the age of 81 without ever knowing who her father was.

▲ *This picture of Emma, Lady Hamilton, hung in Nelson's cabin on HMS* Victory. *It can still be seen there today. Emma was not popular with the British people. Nelson's instructions for her well-being after his death were ignored.*

# Napoleon, Villeneuve, and Gravina

As a British naval commander, Horatio Nelson had to face an enemy that was led by a great soldier. Napoleon Bonaparte had been born in Ajaccio, on the island of Corsica, in 1769. He spoke French with a strong Corsican accent all his life. After military school, he joined the army and became an officer in the artillery.

After the French Revolution of 1789, there was a period of chaos and violence. Each new set of rulers tried to bring in new ideas and to become powerful. Amid the uncertainty, Napoleon became popular very quickly. Like many soldiers, he saw things in simple terms. He believed in good organization and tough discipline. He had the will to get any job done quickly and well. Napoleon had a good memory for detail and kept close control of many things himself.

## Napoleon as emperor

Napoleon brought the period of chaos in France to an end. He made taxes and laws much simpler, and brought in many new ones. Many of the laws still in force in European countries today were first drawn up by Napoleon. He built better roads, which could be used by his armies.

However, Napoleon wanted power and glory for himself and his family, and this was not always good for France. It was only 15 years after the French king had been overthrown that Napoleon had himself crowned emperor in the cathedral of Notre Dame in Paris.

▶ *Napoleon was crowned emperor in December 1804. The splendid service in Notre Dame Cathedral was led by Pope Pius VII.*

# TRAFALGAR

◀ *Admiral Pierre Villeneuve (left) was the commander in chief of all the French and Spanish ships at Trafalgar. The Spanish ships of the combined fleet were commanded by an Italian, Don Federico Gravina (right).*

Napoleon wanted to win new land for France and he saw Britain as an ancient enemy of his country. He ordered many new ships to be built in order to invade Britain. These included large, flat-bottomed ships called *prames*. They were designed to sail close to the shore and up rivers. However, the French naval minister, Admiral Denis Decrès, had an impossible task in preparing the ports for such a huge fleet. It never sailed.

## Pierre Villeneuve

What kind of a man was Pierre Villeneuve, the commander of the French battle fleet at this time? He came from the south of France and had joined the navy at the age of 15, when Louis XV was still king. As a young man he was successful in battle and was promoted quickly.

Unlike Nelson, Villeneuve was not a keen supporter of his government. He disagreed with many of Napoleon's plans. He even ignored some of Napoleon's orders and had failed to join the fleet that was supposed to invade Britain.

## The Spanish commander

The alliance between France and Spain dated back to October 1803. France had convinced Spain that Britain was a serious threat to Spanish rule in the West Indies. Napoleon welcomed the increase in his fleet and the use of Spanish as well as French ports.

The Spanish fleet was commanded by Don Federico Gravina. He was actually an Italian, born in Sicily, but he had close links to the Spanish royal family. He went to the coronation of Napoleon in 1804 and became an admiral in the same year. He met and gained the respect of Admiral Decrès at this time. However, Villeneuve and Gravina never got along. The French commander was quiet and thoughtful, while Gravina was an energetic man who loved to see action.

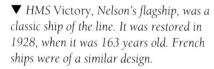

# Ships of the line

Warships at the time of Trafalgar were made of wood. The timbers of the keel were made of oak; elm was also used. Below the waterline, the **hull** was plated with copper. This protected it from the teredo worm, which bores into ships' timbers.

HMS *Victory* was built as a "First-Rate Ship of the Line," which meant that it was designed for battle. It was launched at Chatham in 1765. The ship weighed 2,162 tons and was only 226 ft (69 meters) long. Even so, it carried 104 guns and had a crew of 850 men. HMS *Victory* was Nelson's flagship when he sailed to Trafalgar from the English Channel port of Portsmouth in 1805.

A ship of the line like HMS *Victory* had three tall masts. The first was the **foremast** and the second was the **mainmast**. The rear mast was called the **mizzen**. All three were fitted, or rigged, with a range of canvas sails. The *Victory* carried more than three complete sets of sails, which amounted to 172,160 sq ft (16,000 square meters).

The sails were **unfurled** and **furled**, or let out and taken in, by sailors who had to climb high up the masts and struggle with the ropes. Men also went aloft to act as lookouts, and **sharpshooters** sometimes climbed the mast to fire at the enemy in battle.

▼ HMS Victory, *Nelson's flagship, was a classic ship of the line. It was restored in 1928, when it was 163 years old. French ships were of a similar design.*

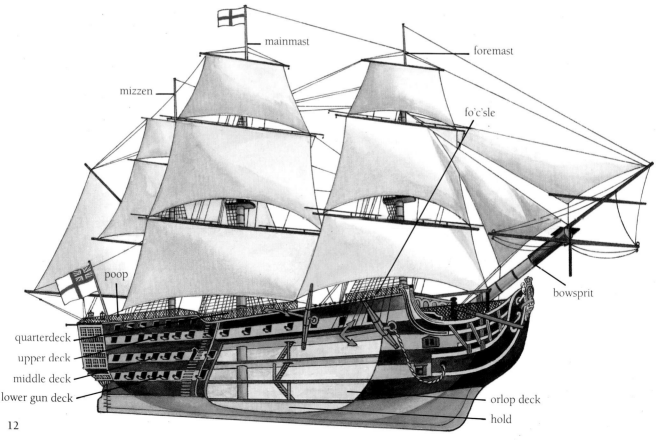

# TRAFALGAR

LAUNCHED AT CHATHAM DOCKYARD 7TH. MAY 1765.
EXTREME LENGTH 226'-6"    LENGTH OF KEEL 151'-3"
EXTREME BEAM 52'-6"    DEPTH OF HOLD 21'-6"
LENGTH OF GUN DECK 186'    TONNAGE 2162 TONS, DISPLACEMENT TONNAGE 3500TONS
ARMAMENT.
LOWER DECK 30 LONG 32 PDR.  MIDDLE DECK 30 LONG 24 PDR.  MAIN DECK 32 LONG 12 PDR.  UPPER DECK 12 SHORT 12 PDR.

◀ *Details about the dimensions of HMS* Victory *are painted on a panel on the lower gun deck. It is interesting to compare its size with that of a modern oil tanker. The Seawise Giant (1976–1988) was the largest tanker ever built. It was more than 6.5 times as long as HMS* Victory, *and more than 255 times as heavy. However, the tanker had a crew of only 25–30 men and women, while the* Victory *carried 850 men.*

Ropes ran from the steering wheel to the **stern** of the ship. There, they shifted a beam called the **tiller**. This in turn moved the **rudder**, which steered the ship. When the ship needed to stop, two huge anchors were lowered. They dug into the seabed and held the ship still.

On a ship like HMS *Victory* there were seven decks, or levels. Uppermost at the stern was an open deck called the **poop**. This was the best place to get a view of the surrounding sea. Toward the front of the ship, or **bow**, lay another open deck. This was used for exercise and recreation by the crew. Its old-fashioned name, the forecastle, had by now been shortened to **foc's'le**.

The **quarterdeck** was where the ship's officers stood to command the ship's movements and actions. It lay **amidships**.

Farther down was the airy upper **gun deck** and then the middle gun deck. At the stern of these levels were the officers' quarters. On the *Victory* these included Nelson's day cabin and dining room. The lower gun deck was home to most of the crew for months on end. They had to share the crowded space with the cannons and with the live animals carried on board for meat. They slept in swaying **hammocks**.

Below was the dark and cramped **orlop** (overlap) deck. It was here that the ship's surgeon carried out operations and amputations during battle. Finally came the ship's **hold**. This contained supplies of dried food for long voyages, as well as powder and shot for the cannons.

Six hundred to eight hundred men had to put up with the cramped, dark living quarters during the voyage. Ships were lit only by candles or oil lamps. Food and water had to be stored without refrigeration.

There was no radio or telephone. Ships communicated with one another by hoisting flag signals. A letter from London providing information about the enemy might take two months to reach the Mediterranean Sea.

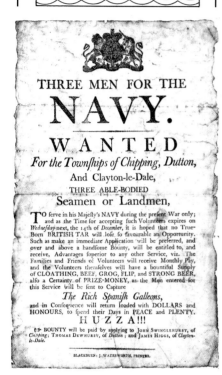

*A poster calls on men to join the British Royal Navy. Few took up the offer willingly. They preferred to sail on trading vessels.*

# A sailor's life

For many years before the Battle of Trafalgar, Britain, France, and Spain had known war or the threat of war. In 1701 there had been only 30,000 men in the British Royal Navy. By 1805, 120,000 sailors were needed to defend the country. Recruiting men to join the navy was difficult. Few men chose a career on a warship, where life was hard and discipline was harsh. There was considerable risk of death from disease or in battle.

## Joining the crew

Men who went to sea preferred the easier life of the **merchant navy**, where pay and conditions were better. However, in times of war the British government ordered the captains of the merchant fleet to dismiss, or **stand down**, their crews. As the merchant sailors left their ships, naval recruiting officers and **press gangs** would waylay the sailors and force them to join up in the fighting service.

Four weeks before Trafalgar, the French fleet was short 2,000 men. Many were ill or were missing. The press gangs in Cadiz were very harsh.

In the British navy sailors received a monthly wage of 23 shillings and sixpence (about $2.00). From this they had to buy and make their own clothes, for no uniform was issued. They were often paid nothing until they returned to port.

For some crew members, life on board was the lesser of two evils. Many sailors were foreigners escaping justice in their own countries. There were convicted criminals from Britain. Some found the life on board less harsh than in jails, although conditions in both were very bad.

Officers on board had much better lives, but many had been at sea from the age of 12 or even younger.

## Food and drink

Ships of this period were often at sea for months at a time. Live bullocks and sheep were carried on board and these were killed during the voyage so that the officers could have fresh meat to eat.

Most of the crew ate only tough meat or fish, preserved by salting or drying, and hard ship's biscuit. Because there was no refrigeration, worms and maggots would often attack the food. Sometimes the meat was boiled up in a soup to soften it—and to hide the extra creatures!

It was difficult to keep water fresh. Weevils and maggots would infest this too. Men were allowed to drink rough wine or, when in port, up to a gallon (4.5 liters) of beer a day. In the tropics a ration of rum mixed with water, known as "grog," was given to all crew members at the midday and evening meals. For many years a daily tot of rum was standard issue to all men in the Royal Navy.

# TRAFALGAR

◀ *A press gang in London in 1780, when Nelson was a 22-year-old post-captain. Press gangs did not invite men to serve in the navy—they forced them. Sometimes press gangs found people who were suspected of crimes. They threatened to tell all if these people would not join up.*

## Disease

Keeping healthy on board ship was always a problem. On tropical voyages many sailors would die from yellow fever. Lack of fresh fruit and vegetables caused a disease called scurvy, although Nelson always did his best to get fresh food for his men.

No one could escape the constant wet and the dampness, and many suffered from painful attacks of rheumatism. Battles at sea were bloody affairs, but in Nelson's day 13 times as many men died from diseases as were killed in battle.

## Discipline and punishment

The 600 crew members on the lower gun deck had to live very closely with one another. Each man was given only 14 inches (35 centimeters) of space—the width of his body—in which to hang his hammock. Quarrels and fights could break out, and discipline was needed every day, not just during battle.

Discipline was extremely harsh. **Desertion** or **mutiny** were punished by hanging. Drunkenness or disobedience were punished by a flogging. Thirty-six lashes were given with a **cat-o'-nine-tails**. This was a rope, one end of which was separated out into strands. A lead pellet was melted into each of these strands. After each flogging the ship's surgeon would rub salt into the open wounds to prevent infection.

It says a lot for Nelson's character that, despite such conditions, the crew was loyal to his command. The men knew that Nelson had had a lifetime's experience of hardship at sea. They also respected his **patriotism**. A junior officer wrote that Nelson "was adored and, in fighting under him, every man thought himself sure of success."

### Maggots and wine

An 11-year-old midshipman describes the food on board:

"We live on meat which has been 10 or 11 years in the cask and on biscuits which make your throat cold in eating it owing to the maggots which are very cold when you eat them! Being like calf's foot jelly or blomange [blancmange] . . . We drink wine which is exactly like bullock's blood and sawdust mixed together."

# Fighting at sea

All the skills of seamanship were needed to bring ships together in battle. A change of wind direction or strength could change the course of the battle completely. Rising and falling tides affected the ship's movements in harbor.

At the time when Nelson was commander on HMS *Victory*, the custom was for ships to sail in two parallel lines. This was the **order of sailing**. When fighting, the ships moved into **order of battle**, strung out in a single line. The enemy formed a similar line. The short range of cannon fire meant that ships had to come close alongside in order to fight.

On several occasions Nelson broke with this formation. He sailed into battle with two or three parallel lines of ships. He broke up the enemy line and isolated groups of their ships.

The first aim was to disable an enemy ship so that it could not sail away. Cannon fire destroyed the masts and sails. The attacker could then board the enemy ship and fight the crew.

A captured vessel, with prisoners below deck and precious cargo in its hold, was of much greater value than a sunken wreck. It could be repaired and sent to sea again. The *Raisonnable*, on which Nelson first went to sea, was a ship captured from the French.

Sailors carried muskets, pistols, and swords for hand-to-hand fighting with the enemy during boarding or defense.

Since 1750 the cannon had been the main battle weapon. These guns were referred to by the weight of cannonball that they could fire. A 32-pounder could fire a 32-pound (14.5-kilogram) cannonball. Cannonballs could be heated until they were very hot and then fired very low so that they would start fires in the hull of the enemy ship.

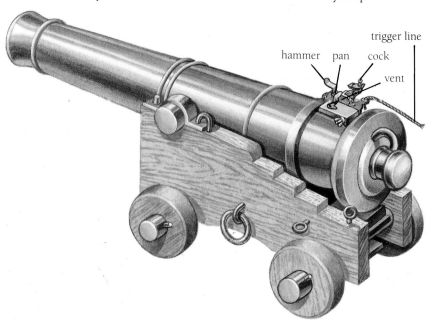

trigger line

hammer   pan   cock

vent

▶ *Cannons were heavy iron guns mounted on wheels. They were rolled forward before firing. The force of the discharge made them fly backward. They were secured with ropes.*

# TRAFALGAR

◀ *Nelson receives the sword of the Spanish admiral after the Battle of Cape St. Vincent in 1797. This was a sign of surrender. Nelson deliberately disobeyed orders at this battle. He broke out of line toward seven Spanish ships and boarded two of them.*

Other missiles were also fired by cannons. **Barshot** was fired to rip sails and smash masts. **Fagotshot** and **grapeshot** were made up of clusters of iron shot that exploded on impact and were designed to kill and wound as many men as possible. At Trafalgar, short, light iron cannons called **carronades** fired very heavy shots at close range. These took longer to reload, but could be moved around the ship more easily.

## Preparing for battle

Even today people often say they want to "clear the decks for action." Originally, this was the order given to sailors before a battle. They had to work fast and hard to get ready in time. Furniture and bedding were put away and windows removed. Sails were secured and safety nets were put up to catch falling men and debris. Fire was a terrible risk. A fire in the **galley** would be wetted down and fire buckets prepared.

The decks were covered with wet sand. This prevented men from slipping on blood later in the battle. The ship's boats were made ready for boarding enemy ships, and the guns were prepared.

A crew of 12 men handled each cannon, which could weigh as much as three tons. Everyone stripped to the waist and tied **kerchiefs** around their heads in order to block their ears and muffle the roar of the cannon. The powder boy, sometimes known as the **powder monkey**, was a small and agile member of the gun crew. It was his job to fetch and carry the gunpowder needed during the battle.

The ship's surgeon and carpenter now prepared their station on the orlop deck. Together, they carried out operations during the battle. Smashed limbs were amputated. There was no **anesthetic** to reduce the pain. The patient was given a mouthful of rum to swallow and a leather gag to bite on while the limb was sawed or chopped off. The stump was daubed with hot **pitch** to seal and disinfect the wound. The unhygienic conditions often led to **gangrene**, and death was common.

# Countdown to battle

In 1803, Nelson was living in retirement at Merton Place, an elegant house near London, which he had bought to suit the needs of Emma, Lady Hamilton. This was the year of the uneasy peace. Napoleon was planning the invasion of Britain and working out his plan of enticing the British fleet to the West Indies.

When the peace finally failed, Nelson was appointed commander in chief of the British fleet in the Mediterranean. The coming months were to be spent in the blockade of the French and Spanish fleets. There followed the long chase across the Atlantic Ocean and back again. By August 21, 1805, the combined fleet was back in the Spanish port of Cadiz, despite the fact that Napoleon had ordered Villeneuve to sail northward into the Channel port of Boulogne.

Nelson had been ordered home after two years at sea without a break. On August 20, 1805, when the French and Spanish fleet was approaching Cadiz, he arrived back at Merton Place, where he spent 25 days with Lady Hamilton.

The break was far from restful. People who knew that Nelson was not at sea feared that Britain was not properly guarded. If the immediate threat of invasion was over, it was still likely that the combined forces of France and Spain would launch an attack, perhaps on a British merchant fleet sailing from the West Indies or the Far East.

▲ Nelson spent the summer before Trafalgar at Merton Place, near London, with Emma, Lady Hamilton. This part of the house was known as the "quarterdeck."

## Politics and war

Napoleon never trusted his admirals. Although he was a brilliant soldier, he never really understood the strengths and needs of the French navy. This failure was crucial. It meant that the combined fleet was less well trained than the British and that its ships were less well supplied.

On the other hand, Nelson had the full confidence of the British government. He was supported by the British prime minister, William Pitt the Younger, and by the new secretary of state for war and the colonies, Viscount Castlereagh.

Nelson himself put forward at this time a bold new battle tactic, which became known as the "Nelson Touch." He had complete confidence in his own judgment and in that of his captains. Once, when it was pointed out to him that the combined French and Spanish fleet might number as many as 100 ships, he was asked how many ships of the line the British had at their disposal. He replied carelessly, "Oh, I do not count our ships."

On September 13, 1805, Nelson received his last orders from the Admiralty, the government navy office. He left Merton for Portsmouth to **embark** on HMS *Victory*. He noted in his diary: "Friday night, at half past ten, drove from dear, dear Merton where I left all that I hold dear in this world, to go to serve my king and country." It was the last time that he was ever to see Emma.

# TRAFALGAR

◀ *Five weeks before the Battle of Trafalgar, Nelson traveled to Portsmouth to join HMS* Victory. *The crowds pressed around him. "I had their huzzas (cheers) before," he said. "I have their hearts now."*

## The "Nelson Touch"

"I shall form the fleet into three divisions in three lines. One division shall be composed of twelve or fourteen of the fastest two-decked ships, which I shall always keep to windward, or in a situation of advantage: and I shall put them under an officer who, I am sure, will employ them in the manner I wish, if possible. I consider it will always be in my power to throw them into battle in any part I may choose; but if circumstances prevent their being carried against the enemy where I desire, I shall feel certain he will employ them effectually, and, perhaps, in a more advantageous manner than if he could have followed my orders.

"With the remaining part of the fleet formed in two lines, I shall go at them at once, if I can, about one-third of their line from their leading ship. I think it will surprise and confound the enemy. They won't know what I am about. It will bring forward a pell-mell battle, and that is what I want."

# The fleets prepare

In the next few weeks Nelson made sure the ships were supplied with as much fresh food as possible and all the other stores needed for a voyage and battle.

British ships under the command of Admiral William Cornwallis and Vice Admiral Lord Collingwood had been keeping the French fleet under close observation. Nelson sailed from Portsmouth and joined the British fleet on September 28, 1805. "Saw the enemy's fleet in Cadiz," he noted in his diary, "amounting to thirty-five or thirty-six sail-of-the-line." At no time did Nelson's fleet number more than the enemy.

The French fleet was less well organized. Napoleon was still unwilling to keep his navy properly supplied and was impatient with its commanders. The French emperor had ordered Villeneuve back to Paris and was replacing him as fleet commander with Admiral François-Etienne Rosily. Historians believe that Villeneuve only decided to leave Cadiz in order to avoid the shame of being replaced.

After a week of terrible storms, Friday, October 18 was a clear, warm day. Villeneuve gave orders for the combined fleet to sail. The wind was too light, and it was not until 5:00 A.M. on Saturday that the ships began to appear at the entrance to Cadiz harbor.

## Into stormy seas

Captain Blackwood, on the British **frigate** HMS *Euryalus*, was keeping watch on the combined fleet. At first the leading ships were spread out and appeared to be sailing for the Strait of Gibraltar. Blackwood signaled this information to Nelson, who ordered: "General chase, southeast. Prepare for battle."

Sunday was a dark day, with heavy rain, thick weather, and wind from the south-southwest. The remainder of Villeneuve's fleet managed to leave Cadiz harbor, but it was still in a long, straggling line. It headed southwest, shadowed in the northwest by the British fleet.

Monday, October 21, 1805, dawned cloudy, with a faint breeze. The French had used a new calendar since the Revolution. To them this day was 29 Vendémiaire, in the Revolutionary Year XIV. The combined fleet was strung out in a line nearly 9 miles (15 kilometers) long. Nelson's entire fleet of 31 ships appeared over the northwest horizon. The wind was behind them.

## An unexpected change

At 8:00 A.M. Villeneuve gave an astonishing signal to his fleet—to **wear** together, or face into the wind. They were turning back toward Cadiz and heading north. The winds were light, but there was a deep swell, a sure sign of a storm to come.

No one can say why Villeneuve gave orders to turn back into the

▲ *Conditions in the cramped lower decks during battle were terrifying, with splintering wood, smoke, and heat.*

# TRAFALGAR

path of the approaching British fleet. It turned out to be a suicide mission. Villeneuve's fleet was bigger than Nelson's, but not by enough to give him any confidence. He was having the greatest difficulty keeping his own ships in formation.

Nelson had already raised the "Prepare for Battle" signal. He then made an entry in his diary. It was to be his last: "At daylight saw enemy's combined fleet from east to east-southeast. **Bore** away. Made the signal for order of sailing and to prepare for battle. The enemy with their heads to the southward. At seven the enemy wearing in succession."

Fires were put out and loose furniture and equipment were **stowed**. Live cattle were thrown overboard in case they broke loose and caused confusion during the battle. Gunpowder supplies were opened, and heavy fire curtains of water-soaked felt were put into place. Hand weapons were issued to the crews. The men had a last meal of meat, cheese, and wine or grog.

Nelson made an addition to his will entrusting Emma Hamilton to the care of his country, and then made a last prayer to God.

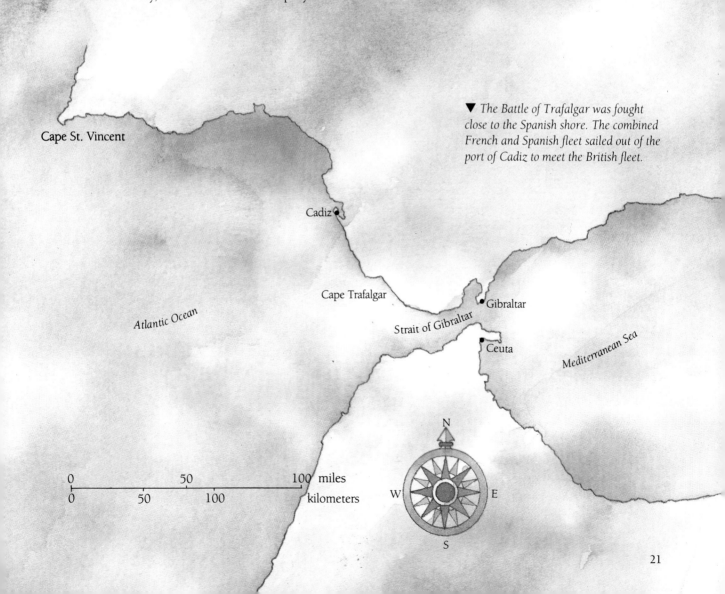

▼ *The Battle of Trafalgar was fought close to the Spanish shore. The combined French and Spanish fleet sailed out of the port of Cadiz to meet the British fleet.*

Cape St. Vincent

Cadiz

Cape Trafalgar

Gibraltar

Strait of Gibraltar

Ceuta

Atlantic Ocean

Mediterranean Sea

| 0 | 50 | 100 miles |

| 0 | 50 | 100 kilometers |

N
W E
S

# "England expects..."

Nelson had been confused by the enemy's sudden change of direction. The British fleet was now sailing directly toward the French and Spanish in two lines. Nelson could not tell which ship was Villeneuve's. The enemy fleet was straggling along in groups. The weather stayed cloudy, with a breeze from the west-northwest.

## A famous signal

By 11:25 A.M., only 1.75 miles (3 kilometers) separated the two fleets. Nelson said to Lieutenant John Pasco, "I will now amuse the fleet with a signal. Mr. Pasco, I wish to say 'England confides [is confident] that every man will do his duty.'"

Pasco looked up the flag signals in the new code book produced by Sir Home Popham. Flags could be used to stand for single letters or for whole words. Pasco replied, "If your Lordship will permit me to substitute 'England expects,' the signal will be sooner completed, since the words are in the vocabulary and the others must be spelt."

Nelson replied, "That will do, Pasco. Send it directly." After that, the flags for code number 16 were hoisted: "Engage the enemy more closely."

▲ These flags made up the most famous signal in British naval history. Separate flags were needed for the letters of the word duty.

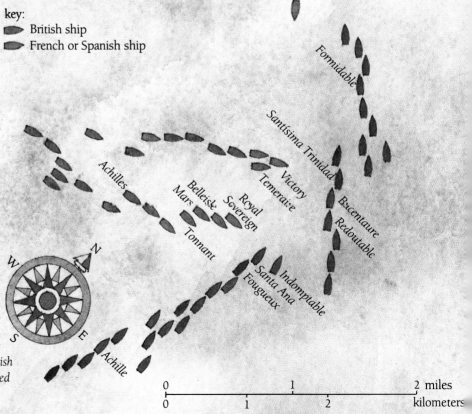

key:
British ship
French or Spanish ship

▶ The position of the two fleets at 12:00 noon on the day of battle. The British ships form two battle lines. The combined fleet forms one long, straggling line.

# TRAFALGAR

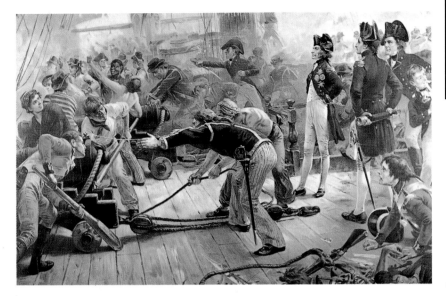

◀ *At the height of the battle, Nelson stood on the quarterdeck of HMS* Victory. *His medals could be seen clearly. He was an obvious target for enemy sharpshooters.*

## The battle begins

Nelson's flagship was at the head of the line of ships with the wind behind them. The *Victory's* captain was Thomas Masterman Hardy. Captain Eliab Harvey of HMS *Temeraire* felt that he should lead so that the flagship and its commander would be at less risk. Nelson disagreed. Vice Admiral Cuthbert Collingwood, on the *Royal Sovereign*, led the line of ships on the more sheltered side. This column was heading for those enemy ships sailing behind the leading groups.

Shortly before noon the French ships opened fire on the *Victory*. The first shots either fell short or overshot, but soon the flagship was in the direct line of fire. The *Victory* was hit on the sixth try and then seven or eight French ships poured **broadsides** into the side of the flagship.

Nelson's secretary, John Scott, and Captain Hardy's clerk, Thomas Whipple, were both killed instantly. The top of the mizzen mast was shot away. The sails were riddled with holes. The wheel that steered the ship was blown to pieces and sailors had to steer the ship directly from the tiller at the stern. Nelson was heard to say to his captain, "This is too warm work, Hardy, to last long."

So far, the *Victory* had not fired a single shot. Nelson's main aim was to pretend to be attacking the front ships in the enemy line. This would give Collingwood the best chance of making his attack. Collingwood was now under heavy fire, too, as he attacked the *Santa Ana*, the *Indomptable*, and the *Fougueux*. A broadside from the *Royal Sovereign* killed and wounded many of the Spanish gun crew on the *Santa Ana*.

At this point, Captain Hargood on the *Belleisle* and two other British ships, the *Mars* and the *Tonnant*, came to help Collingwood. The *Belleisle* came under fierce attack from the French 74-gun *Achille*. At one stage it looked as if the *Belleisle* would be forced to surrender. In the end, no British ship was either sunk or captured. All ships were badly damaged and the *Belleisle* was totally dismantled.

# A musket shot

The fierce attacks on the *Victory* continued, with the French ship *Redoutable* firing broadsides into it. Darkness would fall at about 5:00 P.M., and both sides knew that the battle had to be decided by then.

At 1:00 P.M., Villeneuve's flagship, the *Bucentaure*, came under fire from the *Victory*. Captain Hardy had ordered the carronades into action. The 68-pounders fired their 68-pound (30-kilogram) cannonballs and kegs packed with 500 musket balls at almost point-blank range. There was terrible death and destruction on the French ship.

Nelson's aim was still to cut through the enemy line and board one of the French ships. Hardy thought this would be too difficult, as the enemy ships were so close together—"closed as a forest" were his words. Nelson brushed this aside, adding that it did not matter which of the ships was boarded. "Take your choice," he said.

Having passed the *Bucentaure*, Hardy maneuvered the British flagship alongside the *Redoutable*, which had been causing such damage. The two ships crashed into each other, locked in a death grip. Their anchors struck each other and their sails tangled. Some of the fire was taken by the nearby *Temeraire* and the huge Spanish ship *Santisima Trinidad*, but the *Redoutable* still had sharpshooters and grenade throwers aloft. They were used to deadly effect.

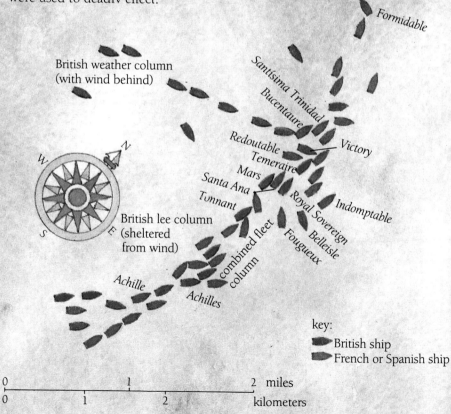

British weather column
(with wind behind)

Formidable

Santisima Trinidad

Bucentaure

Redoutable

Temeraire

Victory

Mars

Santa Ana

Tunnant

Royal Sovereign

Indomptable

British lee column
(sheltered from wind)

Belleisle

Fougueux

combined fleet column

Achille

Achilles

key:
British ship
French or Spanish ship

0    1    2 miles
0    1    2 kilometers

▶ *The position of the fleets at 1:15 P.M. on the day of battle. The British ships engaged the enemy more closely, following Nelson's orders.*

# TRAFALGAR

## An easy target

Nelson continued to walk the quarterdeck with Captain Hardy. They were completely in the open. Nelson wore his admiral's uniform coat, with the four stars of his knighthood on the left breast. Hardy and the other officers had urged him to wear something different or to cover up the stars with a handkerchief. Nelson had agreed, but added: "It is too late now to be shifting a coat."

At 1:25 P.M. a sharpshooter fired a musket from the mizzen mast of the *Redoutable*. A deadly ball the size of a cherry pierced Nelson's golden **epaulette**. It entered his lung and lodged itself in his spine. Nelson fell to the deck. Supporting himself on his one arm, he said, "Hardy, I believe they have done it at last."

The battle continued to rage all around him.

▼ *Nelson lies on deck, shot through his lung by an enemy sharpshooter. Captain Hardy is at his side. As the battle raged, Nelson was carried below decks.*

# Victory and death

N elson's backbone was shot through. He was taken down to the orlop deck, which was painted red to conceal the blood shed in battle. A handkerchief covered his face. He was anxious that the crew should not see him and be discouraged. Nelson was sure he would die quickly, but he lived for three more hours. In great pain, he was given lemonade and fanned to keep him cool. Even as he lay dying, he was kept informed of the progress of the battle.

Part of the combined French and Spanish fleet, under Rear Admiral Pierre Dumanoir on the 80-gun *Formidable*, had continued to sail in a northeasterly direction, away from the scene of battle. It was only at 2:30 P.M., when the battle was practically lost, that the *Formidable* began to turn back to the action.

Meanwhile, at the rear of the line, the British ship *Achilles* was fighting an enemy ship with the same name, in French *Achille*. At 4:30 P.M. the guns of HMS *Prince* shot down the mainmast of the *Achille*. As dusk fell, the ship became a blazing wreck. British boats rowed in close, trying to save the French crew from being burned alive. At 5:45 P.M. the fire reached stored gunpowder and the *Achille* exploded. Some 500 men died. By this point eleven other ships from this 19-strong section of the combined fleet had been captured, while seven had sailed off.

▲ *The musket ball that killed Nelson was later mounted in crystal and presented to Mr. Beatty, the ship's surgeon. The clasp is kept today at Windsor Castle.*

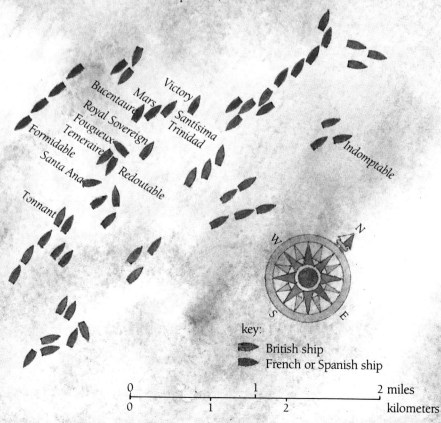

▶ *The position of the two fleets at 4:30 P.M. Nelson has just died and the British have won the battle. The combined fleet is in chaos.*

key:
◣ British ship
◗ French or Spanish ship

0         1        2 miles
0    1    2    kilometers

# TRAFALGAR

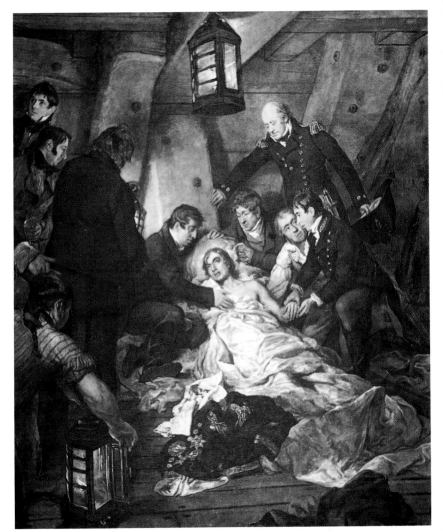

◀ *Horatio Nelson died on the orlop deck of HMS* Victory. *This painting shows him surrounded by his fellow officers, including the ship's surgeon, William Beatty, and the tall figure of Captain Hardy. In reality the orlop deck was far more cramped, being only 5 ft 3 in (1.6 meters). It was dark and wretched. Today this painting, by A. W. Devis, hangs in the ship at the spot where Nelson died.*

## The death of Nelson

Since 4:00 P.M. it had been obvious that the battle had been won by the British fleet. Nelson knew it, although he was very close to death. Captain Hardy congratulated him on his victory, adding unwisely: "I suppose My Lord Admiral Collingwood will take upon himself the direction of affairs." Nelson replied, "Not while I live, I hope, Hardy."

Nelson's last orders were for the fleet to anchor after the battle. He felt sure a storm was coming. In the event, Collingwood ignored this order. As a result, only four of the vessels captured by the British fleet were saved. The rest were blown away by gales. Many were smashed to pieces on the rocks around Cape Trafalgar, adding to the already high death toll.

When people died at sea they were normally buried by being dropped over the side. Nelson was very keen not to go this way, and kept saying "Not over the side, Hardy, not over the side." Nelson's last words have often been misquoted. "God bless you, Hardy," he said, and later, "Thank God I have done my duty." He died at about 4:30 P.M.

### A sad day

"All the men in our ship who have seen him are such soft toads they have done nothing but blast their eyes and cry ever since he was killed."

Seaman on HMS *Victory* after the death of Nelson

# After Trafalgar

The storms that Nelson had forecast made the day after the battle even more miserable. The conditions aboard the damaged ships must have been terrible, with hundreds of sick and wounded men struggling on the decks. The remaining ships of the combined fleet returned to Cadiz, where they were blockaded by Collingwood. Pierre Villeneuve was held prisoner on his own ship, the *Bucentaure*.

## News of the battle

Four days after the battle, HMS *Victory* was towed into Gibraltar. The **schooner** HMS *Pickle* was sent to England at once with the news. Two officers reached Portsmouth on November 5, 1805, and immediately took a fast carriage to London. They arrived in thick fog early the next morning and told their news to Lord Barham of the Admiralty and to the prime minister, William Pitt.

There was no doubt that the battle was a decisive naval victory for Britain. However, the *Annual Register* summed up the feeling of many people in Britain at the time: "There is not an individual who did not feel the victory was purchased at too dear a rate."

In France, Napoleon could not accept the defeat. He silenced all news of Trafalgar until December 7, 1805, when he was also able to announce a remarkable victory for the French army at Austerlitz. Even then, the *Journal de Paris* managed to describe the Battle of Trafalgar as a "brilliant achievement."

The badly damaged *Victory* sailed into Portsmouth on December 4, its flag at half-mast. On December 22 it reached the Thames estuary, carrying Nelson's body. This had been preserved in a barrel of spirits.

*The LONDON GAZETTE EXTRAORDINARY.*
WEDNESDAY, NOV 6, 1805.

ADMIRALTY-OFFICE, Nov. 6.
Dispatches, of which the following are Copies, were received at the Admiralty this day, at one o'clock A. M. from Vice-Admiral Collingwood, Commander in Chief of his Majesty's ships and vessels off Cadiz :—

SIR, *Euryalus*, off Cape Trafalgar, Oct. 22, 1805.
The ever-to-be-lamented death of Vice-Admiral Lord Viscount Nelson, who, in the late conflict with the enemy, fell in the hour of victory, leaves to me the duty of informing my Lords Commissioners of the Admiralty, that on the 19th instant, it was communicated to the Commander in Chief, from the ships watching the motions of the enemy in Cadiz, that the Combined Fleet had put to sea; as they sailed with light winds westerly, his Lordship concluded their destination was the Mediterranean, and immediately made all sail for the Streights' entrance, with the British Squadron, consisting of twenty-seven ships, three of them sixty-fours, where his Lordship was informed, by Captain Blackwood (whose vigilance in watching, and giving notice of the enemy's movements, has been highly meritorious), that they had not yet passed the Streights.

▲ *News traveled slowly in the early 1800s. It was two weeks before the* Times *printed the dramatic news from Trafalgar on its front page.*

▶ *Nelson's funeral procession was very long. The first mounted soldiers had reached St. Paul's Cathedral before the rest of the men had left the Admiralty. For the first part of the journey, Nelson's body was carried by barge along the Thames River from Greenwich.*

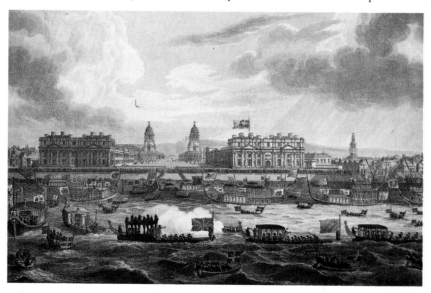

# TRAFALGAR

## The end of an age

On January 9, 1806, 80 days after his death, Horatio Nelson was buried on a day of brilliant sunshine in St. Paul's Cathedral, London. A long funeral procession wound through the streets of London until darkness fell. The men of the *Victory*, who had been carrying the flag-covered coffin, tore off the largest flag and kept pieces of the cloth as souvenirs.

It was in April 1806 that Nelson's old enemy, Villeneuve, was returned to France by his captors. He was soon discovered in a hotel in Rennes, dead. He had six deep knife wounds in and around his heart. Had he killed himself? Or was it murder? Perhaps Napoleon's displeasure at the French defeat had finally caught up with his unfortunate admiral.

Napoleon went on to one famous victory after another. However, he fell from power in 1814 and was finally defeated by the British and Prussian armies at Waterloo, in Belgium, in 1815.

## Nelson remembered

Today a statue of Horatio Nelson stands on top of a tall column in Trafalgar Square, in the heart of London. Many museums, such as Britain's National Maritime Museum at Greenwich, have paintings and other mementos of Nelson's life.

However, the best place to discover how Nelson and his crew lived and died is on board HMS *Victory* itself. The old flagship, fully restored, may still be visited in the docks at Portsmouth, which Nelson knew so well.

▼ *In 1814, Napoleon was exiled to the Mediterranean island of Elba, but he soon returned to France. Defeated by the British and the Prussians at Waterloo in 1815, he was finally exiled to St. Helena in the South Atlantic Ocean. Here he stands on the deck of the Bellerophon, bound for the remote island. He died there six years later at the age of 52.*

# Glossary

**amidships:** the middle part of a ship

**amputate:** to cut off a limb

**anesthetic:** a drug to deaden feeling during an operation

**barshot:** lengths of iron fired from cannon

**bear:** to turn away at sea

**blockade:** to prevent ships entering or leaving a port

**bow:** the front end of a ship

**broadside:** the firing of all the guns on one side of a ship of war at the same time

**carronade:** a kind of giant cannon, first made in Carron, Scotland

**cat-o'-nine-tails:** a rope whip once used to punish sailors in the British navy

**colonist:** someone who lives in a settlement that is not in his or her own country

**compass:** a magnetic needle that points to the north

**desertion:** leaving the armed services without permission

**embark:** to go on board ship

**empire:** a group of countries brought together under a single ruler

**epaulette:** an ornament worn on the shoulder as part of a military uniform

**estuary:** the mouth of a river

**fagotshot:** clusters of uneven pieces of iron shot fired from a cannon

**flagship:** the ship that carries an admiral or other officer commanding a fleet

**fleet:** a large group of ships, such as a navy or a part of it

**foc's'le:** (forecastle) an upper deck at the front of a ship

**foremast:** the front mast on an old sailing vessel

**frigate:** a small, fast warship

**furl:** to roll up a sail or flag

**galley:** a ship's kitchen

**gangrene:** flesh that dies as a result of injury

**grapeshot:** clusters of round iron shot fired from cannon

**gun deck:** any of the decks that carried cannon

**hammock:** a hanging bed made from canvas or net

**hold:** storage or cargo space within a hull

**hull:** the frame or body of a ship

**kerchief:** a scarf

**mainmast:** the central mast of an old sailing vessel

**maneuver:** to carry out planned movements of a military tactic

**merchantman:** a trading ship

**merchant navy:** a nation's fleet of trading ships

**midshipman:** a boy or young man serving as a junior officer

**mizzen:** the rear mast of an old sailing vessel

**musket:** a long handgun, later replaced by the rifle

**mutilation:** permanent injury, such as loss of a limb

**mutiny:** a refusal by soldiers or sailors to obey orders

**navigate:** to steer a ship on its course

# TRAFALGAR

**order of battle:** the formation for a fleet attacking the enemy

**order of sailing:** the formation for a fleet when not engaged in battle

**orlop:** (overlap) a deck lying between the gun decks and the hold

**patriotism:** love of one's country

**pitch:** tar

**poop:** the raised afterdeck of a ship

**post-captain:** a naval rank senior to commander but below full captain

**powder monkey:** a boy who carried stores of gunpowder during battle

**press gang:** a group of men employed, under the command of an officer, to force men into service in the navy or army

**quarterdeck:** the upper deck between the mainmast and the poop deck

**rector:** a priest in charge of more than one parish in the Church of England

**republic:** a country in which the government is elected by the people

**rigging:** the ropes used to work the sails, masts, and pulleys on a ship

**rudder:** a hinged, flat piece of wood used to steer ships

**schooner:** a type of fast sailing ship with two or more masts

**sextant:** an instrument for measuring the position of a ship

**sharpshooter:** a marksman, someone trained to shoot a firearm at individuals

**stand down:** to lay off (a crew)

**stern:** the rear end of a ship

**stow:** to put away or store

**tender:** a boat that brings supplies and stores to a ship

**tiller:** the beam that moves a ship's rudder

**unfurl:** to let out a sail or a flag

**wear:** to turn a ship into the wind